KU-320-486

Farming

Gill Tanner and Tim Wood

Photographs by Maggie Murray

Illustrations by Pat Tourret

A & C Black · London

Here are some of the people you will meet in this book.

The Hart family in 1990

The Cook family in 1960

Bill Hart

Linda Hart

Kerry

Lee

David Cook

June Cook

Susan

Linda

Andrew

Lee Hart is the same age as you.
His sister Kerry is eight years old.
What is Lee's mum called?

This is Lee's mum Linda when she
was just nine years old in 1960.
She is with her mum and dad,
her brother and her baby sister.

The Smith family in 1930

Richard Smith

Lucy Smith

May

Jack and June

The Barker family in 1900

Charles Barker

Alice Barker

Fred

Amy and Adam

Harry

Lucy

This is Lee's granny June
when she was just a baby in 1930.
Her brother Jack is looking after her.

This is Lee's great grandma Lucy
when she was six years old in 1900.
Can you see what her sister
and her brothers are called?

How many differences can you spot between these two photographs?

One shows a modern farmer working in his field and the other shows farm workers in a field one hundred years ago.

This book is about farming.

It will help you find out how farming has changed in the last hundred years.

There are eleven mystery objects in this book and you can find out what they are.
They will tell you a lot about people in the past.

Amy Barker used these mystery objects
when she visited a farm in 1900.
The object on the left is made of wood.
It has a flat top which is a little bigger than this page.
The object on the right is made of wood and metal.
You may have something like it at home
but yours is probably made of plastic or metal.
What do you think these objects are?
What do you think Amy used them for?

Turn the page to find out if you are right.

Can you find the mystery objects in this picture?
The Barker family are having a holiday on a farm.
Amy is learning to milk a cow.
Amy sits on a **milking stool**.
She uses a **wooden bucket** to catch the milk.

In 1900 most milking had to be done by hand.
Amy found it was quite difficult to get milk from the cow.
She had to pull and squeeze at the same time.
Her hands soon became tired.

Farm workers used these two mystery objects together.
Both the mystery objects are metal
and have wooden handles.
The larger object is a kind of curved knife.
The blade is about as long as your arm.
Do you know what it was used for?

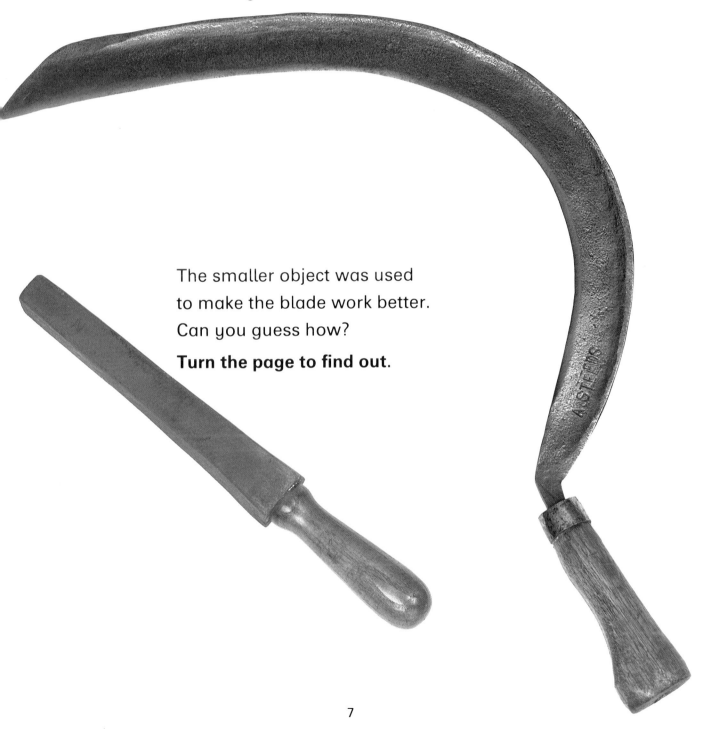

The smaller object was used
to make the blade work better.
Can you guess how?
Turn the page to find out.

Fred is watching the farm workers with their sickles.
One worker swings the **sickle** to cut the wheat.
The other worker rubs the **hone** along the blade
to keep his sickle sharp.
Fred helps by gathering the stalks into bundles.
Each bundle is called a sheaf.
He stands the sheaves in stacks called stooks to dry.

In those days most farm work was done by hand.
There was always lots to do.
Everybody helped at harvest time.

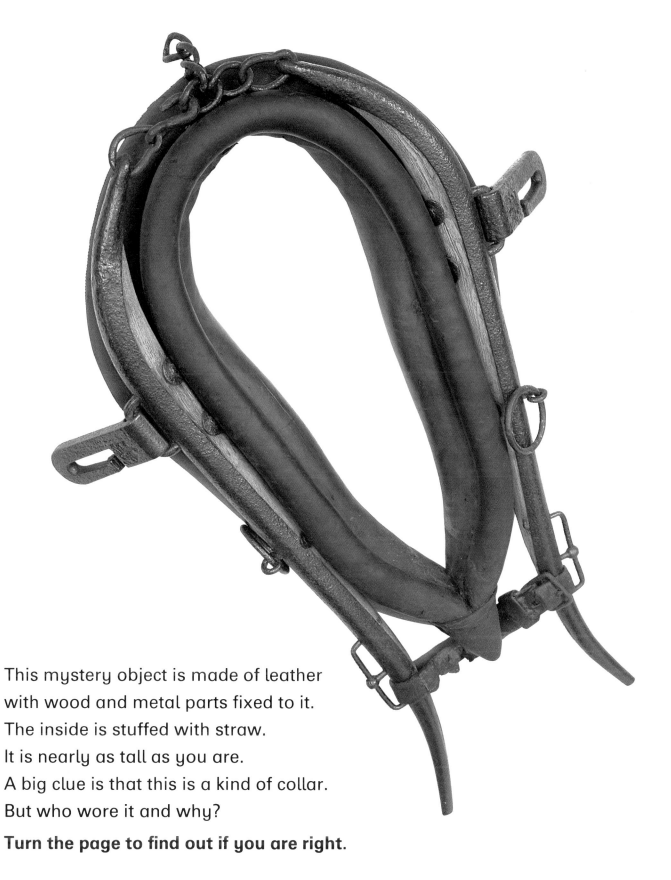

This mystery object is made of leather
with wood and metal parts fixed to it.
The inside is stuffed with straw.
It is nearly as tall as you are.
A big clue is that this is a kind of collar.
But who wore it and why?

Turn the page to find out if you are right.

Amy and Lucy are riding on the hay cart.
Can you see the mystery object in the picture?
It's a **horse collar**.
The collar goes over the horse's head.
The reins the driver uses to guide the horse
run through rings on the top of the collar.
Straps fix the collar to the shafts of the cart.
The collar is padded so the weight of the heavy cart
doesn't hurt the horse's neck.

In 1900 carts and some farm machines
were pulled by horses.
What would a farmer use
to pull heavy loads today?

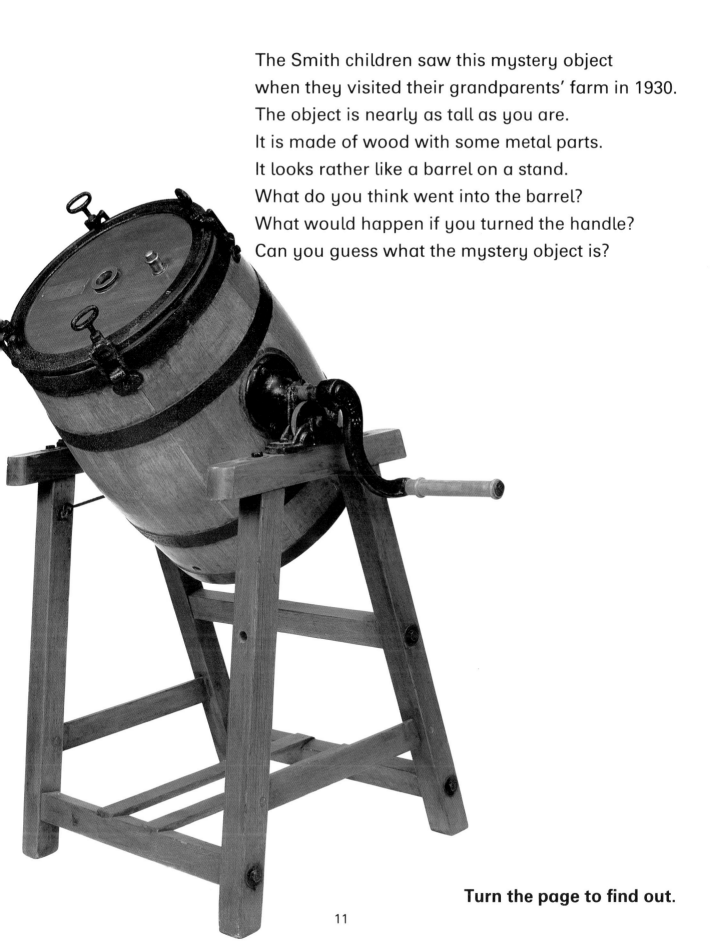

The Smith children saw this mystery object
when they visited their grandparents' farm in 1930.
The object is nearly as tall as you are.
It is made of wood with some metal parts.
It looks rather like a barrel on a stand.
What do you think went into the barrel?
What would happen if you turned the handle?
Can you guess what the mystery object is?

Turn the page to find out.

May and Lucy are in the dairy.
Grandma Smith is showing them how to make butter.
Can you see the mystery object in the picture?
It's a **butter churn**.

Grandma has poured cream into the churn
and fastened the lid tightly.
She shows May how to turn the handle
to make the churn turn over and over.
From time to time Grandma looks through
a glass peephole in the end of the barrel
to see what's happening to the cream.
It takes lots of churning to turn the cream into butter.

These three mystery objects are about the same size
as you see them on the page.
Two of them are made of wood.
One is made of china.
What do you think they are?

Turn the page to see if you are right.

Jack, May and Grandpa are in the kitchen garden.
Can you see the mystery object in the picture?
It is a **seed drill**.

May has put beans in the back of the seed drill.
Jack pushes the seed drill along.
Inside the seed drill, a metal wheel turns
and makes the beans drop out one at a time.
Jack pushes the seed drill along steadily
so that the beans drop out the same distance apart.
Grandpa plants lots of beans each year.
The seed drill puts each bean in the right place.
Grandpa uses a machine like this one, but much bigger
to plant crops in the fields.

16

Linda Cook saw this mystery object
when she visited a farm in 1960.
It is about the same size as an upside-down bucket.
It is made of metal and rubber.
It is a machine which is worked by electricity.
Can you guess what it is?

Turn the page to find out.

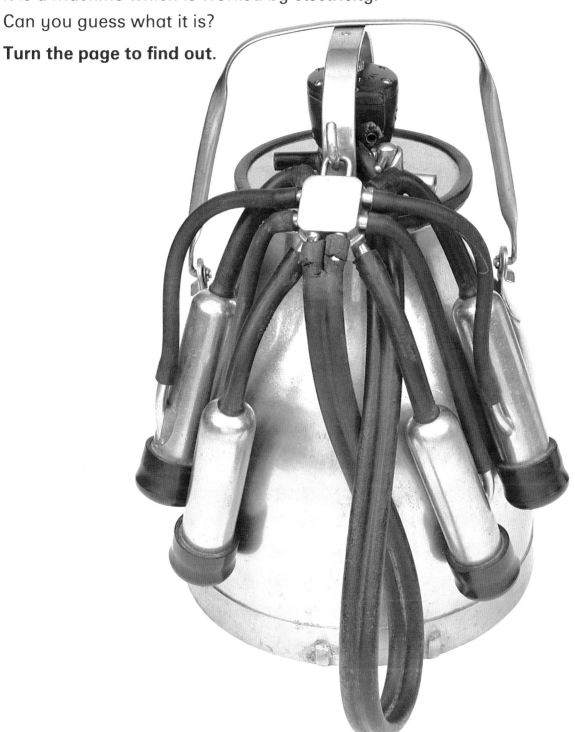

Linda is with the Brownies on a visit to a farm.
The farmer is milking one of his cows.
Can you see the mystery object in the picture?
It is a **milking machine**.

The farmer fits the metal cups over the cow's teats.
The machine sucks the milk from the cow's udder.
The machine doesn't hurt the cow.
It is rather like a calf sucking its mother's milk.
The farmer can milk lots of cows at the same time
using milking machines.

This mystery object has two parts.

One part is made of rubber.

It looks like a big hot water bottle with straps on.

The other part is a rubber tube with a big metal nozzle.

What do you think went into the rubber bag?

What do you think the nozzle is for?

Can you guess what this is?

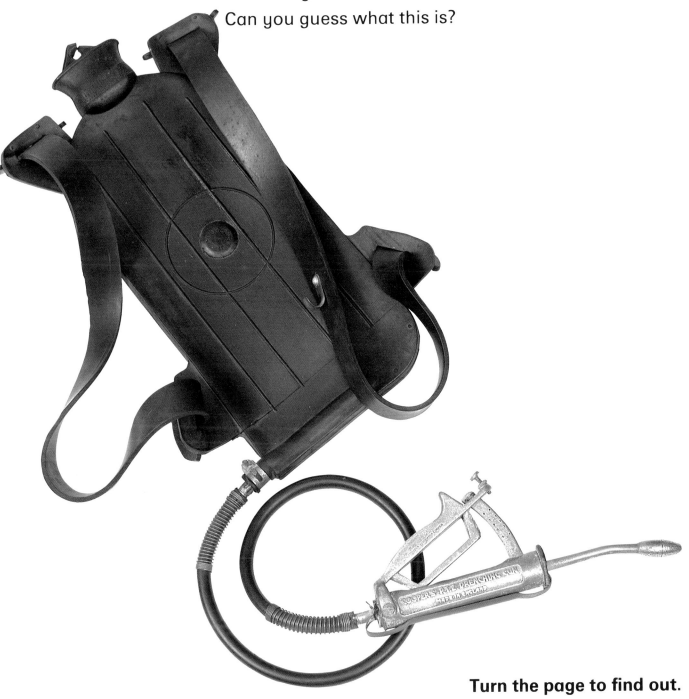

Turn the page to find out.

The Brownies are watching the farmer with his sheep.
Can you see the mystery object in the picture?
It is a **sheep drencher**.

The farmer has to give his sheep some medicine.
He puts the medicine into the rubber bag.
He carries the rubber bag on his back,
with his arms through the straps.
He puts the nozzle into a sheep's mouth
and pulls the trigger to squirt out the medicine.
The farmer can give lots of sheep
exactly the right dose of medicine
with the sheep drencher.

Now that you know a bit more about farming
and how it has changed
over the last hundred years,
see if you can guess
what this mystery object is.

Harry Barker used it on his farm holiday in 1900.
It is about as long as the right-hand page of this book.
It is made of wood.
A big clue is that it makes a noise.
What do you think it is?

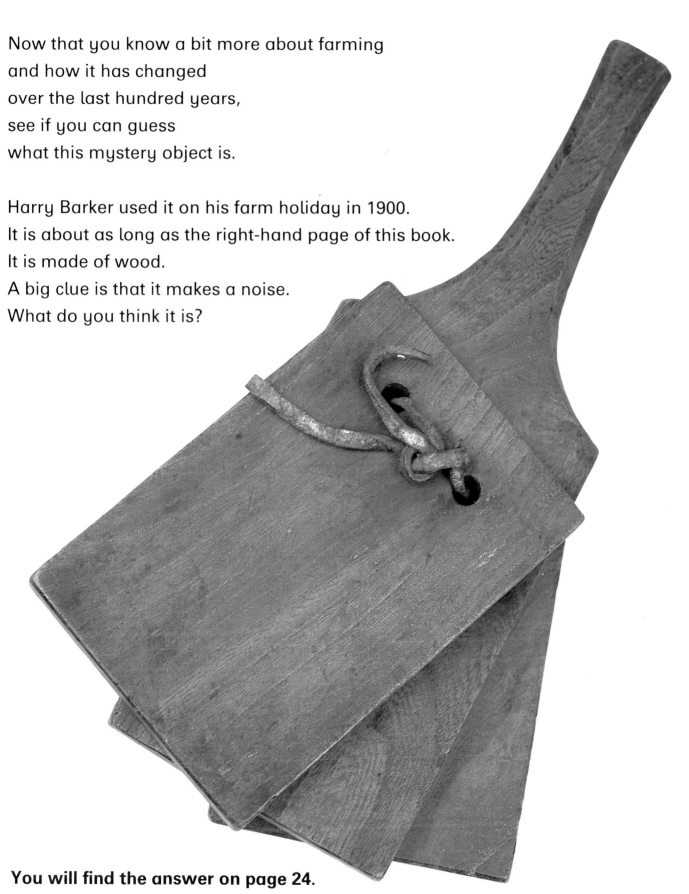

You will find the answer on page 24.

Time-Line

These pages show you the objects in this book and the objects which farmers use nowadays.

1900
The Barker family

wooden bucket

milking stool

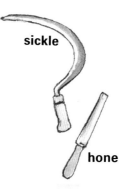

sickle

hone

horse collar

1930
The Smith family

1960
The Cook family

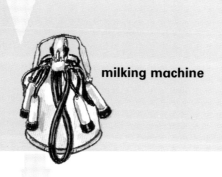

milking machine

1990
The Hart family

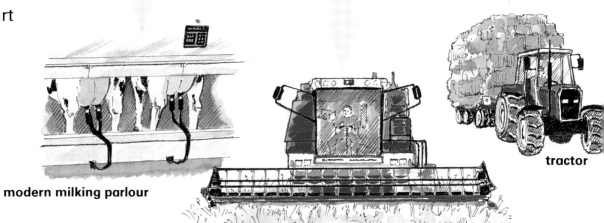

modern milking parlour

combine harvester

tractor

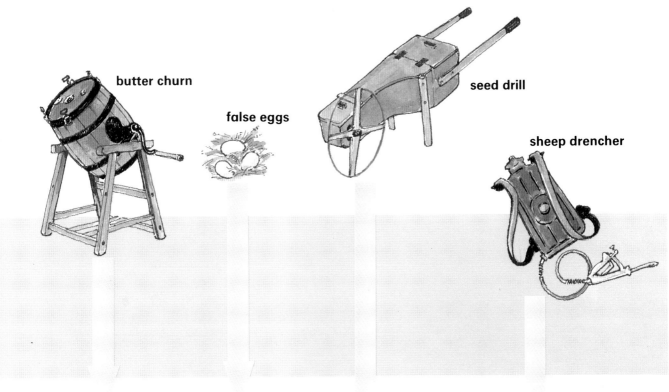

butter churn

false eggs

seed drill

sheep drencher

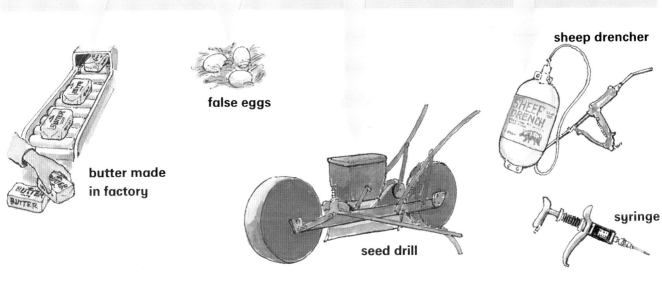

butter made in factory

false eggs

seed drill

sheep drencher

syringe

Index

The **mystery object** on page 21 is a **bird scarer**. When it is shaken the wooden flaps make a loud clacking noise. It was used to scare birds away from crops. This job was often done by children who walked around the fields from dawn to dusk. They made as much noise as they could to frighten birds from newly-planted crops.

For parents and teachers

More about the objects and pictures in this book

Pages 5/6   Bottled milk did not become common until about 1906. Before this time people bought their milk directly from a farmer, a dairy or a milk cart in the street. Customers provided their own containers.

Pages 7/8   The sickle, probably one of the oldest farm tools, has been in use since the Stone Age. The first mechanical reaper was invented in 1799. By 1900, much of the harvest was cut by horse-drawn or steam-powered machines.

Pages 9/10   Horses were first used in agriculture around 2500 BC. The horse collar greatly improved the efficiency of the animal because it allows the horse to pull a large load with greater ease and comfort.

Pages 11/12   It could take about twenty minutes to turn cream to butter by hand churning. Today, most butter is made in factories where, using a continuous churning process, cream can be turned to butter in three minutes.

Pages 13/14   False eggs (also called china, crock, pot or broody eggs) are used mainly to put under broody hens. Most eggs are now produced by battery methods.

Pages 15/16   The horse-drawn seed drill was invented by the Babylonians in about 2000 BC. Mechanical drills, often drawn by tractors, are still used on farms today.

Pages 17/18   The milking machine was invented by Anna Baldwin in the USA in 1878. However, milking machines only gradually replaced hand milking during the first half of the 20th century, because electricity was not widely available.

Pages 19/20   The advantage of the drencher is that it allows many animals to receive a measured dose in a short time. Drenchers are commonly used to treat internal parasites. Sheep can also be treated by injection.

Things to do

History Mysteries will provide an excellent starting point for all kinds of history work. There are lots of general ideas which can be drawn out of the pictures, particularly in relation to the way farming, food, family size and lifestyles have changed in the last 100 years. Below are some starting points and ideas for follow up activities.

1 Work on families and family trees can be developed from the families on pages 2/3, bearing in mind that many children do not come from two-parent, nuclear families. Why do the families in the book have different surnames even though they are related? How have their clothes and hair styles changed over time?

2 Find out about farming in the past from a variety of sources, including books, museums, old postcards, photographs, and, if you live in a farming community, interviews with older people.

3 There is one object which is in one picture of the 1900s, one picture of the 1930s, and one picture of the 1960s. Can you find it?

4 Arrange a field trip to a museum which has exhibits of farming tools from the past. There are also a number of working farm museums and city farms which will allow children to handle animals and look at old and new farming objects.

5 Look at the difference between the photographs and the illustrations in this book. What different kinds of things can they tell you?

6 You may be able to borrow handling collections from your local museum or library service. This is an excellent topic for using outside speakers to recount their experiences of different methods of farming and who can represent different points of view (eg. organic farming compared with intensive farming).

7 Encouraging the children to look at the objects on their visit to a city farm or farming museum is a useful start, but they will get more out of this if you organise some practical activities which will help to develop their powers of observation. Ask the children to make drawings of the objects that they see at the time of their visit, and to collect leaflets or brochures which show pictures of the objects. After returning to the classroom, suggest that one child describes an object to another child, who must then pick out that object from the collection of pictures.

8 After their visit to a museum or city farm, children might make an exhibition of 'before' and 'after' pictures of different farming objects. Talk about each pair of pictures. Some useful questions might be: How can you tell which object is older? Which objects have changed most over time? Why? What do you think of the old objects? How well do you think the objects might work? Is the modern version better than the old version?

9 Make a time-line using your pictures of farming objects. You might find the time-line at the back of this book useful. You could include postcards and photographs in your time-line and other markers to help the children gain a sense of chronology. Use your time-line to bring out the elements of *change* (eg. the increasing use of machines, the use of intensive farming methods, problems of animal welfare, pollution and environmental issues) and *continuity* (eg. the constant need for us to produce food, the cycle of nature and the farming year).

The names and addresses of some organisations which can provide useful information are:

The Butter Council, Education Department, Lime Tree House, 15 Lime Tree Walk, Sevenoaks, Kent TN13 1YH
Tel: (01732 460060)
The National Dairy Council, Education Department, 5–7 John Princes Street, London W1M 0AP Tel: (0171 499 7822)
The Food and Farming Information Service, The National Agricultural Centre, Stoneleigh Park, Warwickshire CV8 2LZ
Tel: (01203 535707)

DUDLEY PUBLIC LIBRARIES

L

702975 | SCH

J630

History Mysteries

First published 1995
A & C Black (Publishers) Limited
35 Bedford Row, London WC1R 4JH

© 1995 A & C Black (Publishers) Limited

ISBN 0-7136-4163-0

A CIP catalogue record for this book is available
from the British Library.

Acknowledgements

The authors and publishers would like to thank Stephen Prince at
the Speed the Plough Collection, Southwell, Nottinghamshire;
Mrs Tanner's Tangible History.

Photographs by Maggie Murray except for:
p.4 (bottom) Sheila Gray/Format Photographers.

All rights reserved. No part of this publication may be used
in any form or by any means – graphic, electronic or
mechanical, including photocopying, recording, taping or
information storage and retrieval systems – without the prior
permission in writing of the publishers.

Filmset by Rowland Phototypesetting Limited, Bury St Edmunds, Suffolk
Printed and bound in the UK by Hunter & Foulis Limited, Edinburgh